Be a
Community
Leader

How to
Organize a Rally

Leslie Harper

PowerKiDS
press
New York

Published in 2015 by The Rosen Publishing Group, Inc.
29 East 21st Street, New York, NY 10010

First Edition

Editor: Norman D. Graubart
Book Design: Joe Carney
Book Layout: Colleen Bialecki
Photo Research: Katie Stryker

Photo Credits: Cover, pp. 5, 17 Fuse/Thinkstock; p. 4 Fotosearch/Archive Photos/Getty Images; p. 6 Paul Thompson/Hulton Archive/Getty Images; p. 7 Universal Images Group/Getty Images; pp. 8, 28 Jupiterimages/Stockbyte/Thinkstock; p. 9 Rich Legg/E+/Thinkstock; p. 10 Michael Smith/Hulton Archive/Getty Images; p. 11 Jamie Grill/Getty Images; p. 13 Rob Hainer/Shutterstock.com; p. 14 Visage/Stockbyte/Getty Images; p. 15 TFoxFoto/Shutterstock.com; p. 16 Jupiterimages/pixland/Thinkstock; p. 18 Pimnana_01/Shutterstock.com; p. 19 Robert Mandel/iStock/Thinkstock; p. 20 Tom Williams/CQ-Roll Call Group/Getty Images; p. 21 JonathanCohen/E+/Getty Images; p. 23 Design Pics/Thinkstock; p. 24 Monkey Business Images/Shutterstock.com; p. 25 Digital Vision/Getty Images; p. 26 Robert Ginn/Photolibrary/Getty Images; p. 27 Sergey Borisov/iStock/Thinkstock; p. 29 Blend Images-Hill Street Studios/Brand X Pictures/Getty Images; p. 30 Blend Images-KidStock/Brand X Pictures/Getty Images.

Library of Congress Cataloging-in-Publication Data

Harper, Leslie.
 How to organize a rally / by Leslie Harper. — 1st ed.
    pages cm. — (Be a community leader)
 Includes index.
 ISBN 978-1-4777-6693-4 (library binding) — ISBN 978-1-4777-6694-1 (pbk.) —
 ISBN 978-1-4777-6695-8 (6-pack)
 1. Demonstrations—Juvenile literature. I. Title.
 HM866.H37 2015
 363.32'3—dc23
                                    2014002970

Manufactured in the United States of America

CPSIA Compliance Information: Batch #WS14PK3: For Further Information contact Rosen Publishing, New York, New York at 1-800-237-9932

Contents

What Is a Rally?

In the United States, people enjoy many important rights and freedoms. Many of these rights are listed in the **Bill of Rights**, which is part of the US Constitution. One very important right mentioned in the Bill of Rights is the right for people to **assemble**, or meet together in groups to express ideas peacefully.

Another word for this type of meeting is a rally. A rally is a large gathering of people who come together for a common purpose. People may hold rallies to protest against laws, or rules, with which they do not agree. They may also hold rallies to raise **awareness** of causes or issues they believe in. Holding a rally is a way to show that large numbers of people support a certain cause. It is also a way to get people together to share information about a cause.

Holding a successful rally takes a lot of planning and organization. With some work, though, a peaceful rally is a great way to get your voice heard and connect with others who support your ideas!

Looking to History

Throughout history, groups of people have used rallies to express ideas. Many successful movements have used rallies to encourage governments to make changes to laws. For example, before 1920, many women in the United States did not have the right to vote in elections. In 1913, about 8,000 women joined in a rally for women's **suffrage** in Washington, DC. The women marched past the White House as people yelled and threw things at them. Many people in the country heard about the rally and began to support the women's cause.

Another famous example is the March on Washington for Jobs and Freedom. This rally was held in Washington, DC, in 1963 and led by Dr. Martin Luther King Jr. More than 200,000 people, most of them African Americans, joined the march to bring attention to the civil rights movement. At this rally, Martin Luther King Jr. gave his famous "I Have a Dream" speech. Less than a year later, the Civil Rights Act of 1964 was passed.

Your Cause

Your cause will be the basis for your rally. Start by looking around your neighborhood. What would you like to change? Maybe you think an empty lot by your school would make a great public park. Maybe a river or lake in your town is polluted and you would like the city government to clean it up. Focus on issues that are important to you and that you feel strongly about.

If you need some help deciding on a cause, talk to your friends and family members. Someone you know may be very passionate about a cause that interests you.

You can also read your local newspaper or attend a town hall or **city council** meeting. This will give you an idea of what others in your town are talking about. You may find you have a strong opinion on a certain issue that you did not know much about before. Offering to organize a rally to bring attention to the issue is a great way to help!

When you have decided on an issue you care about, do some **research** to find out more. Perhaps you learn from the newspaper or a friend that drunk driving has become a serious problem in your town. When people drink too much alcohol, they lose their ability to drive safely. According to Mothers Against Drunk Driving, or MADD, one person is injured every 90 seconds in a drunk-driving accident. Perhaps you hear about a neighbor or friend who was injured in an accident like this. Do more research to find out more about the problem.

As you research drunk driving, you can also find out more about different ways to solve the issue, such as police checkpoints. Find out if your town has a local MADD chapter or a similar organization that fights drunk driving. As you plan your rally, think about what actions you would like to encourage people to take. For example, your rally can encourage people to be designated drivers. Designated drivers drive people who have been drinking home safely.

Location Is Important

Another important decision you will need to make is where to hold your rally. Some rallies, called marches, begin in one place and end in another. This can be an effective way to get people's attention along the way. Marches that go along a public road often require a **permit** from local police, though. For your first rally, you may find it simpler to choose just one location.

When choosing a location, you will want to pick a place where many people will see you. After all, the point of your rally is to show others that an issue has a lot of support, as well as share information about your cause with people passing by. A grocery store or mall parking lot might be a good choice. If your town has a busy park or a town square, try holding your rally there. You will want to pick a place where many people pass through each day. If a goal of your rally is to get local government to take action or change a law, consider holding your rally in front of city hall.

13

In addition to finding a place with a lot of people, you may want to choose a location that relates to your issue. For example, you might choose to hold your rally against drunk driving near the site of a recent drunk-driving accident.

Once you have chosen a location, contact the owner of the property and ask for permission to hold your rally there. You should be prepared to explain the purpose of your rally. You should also be prepared to answer any questions the person or company may have, such as the number of people expected to participate and how long the rally will last.

Because different cities have different rules, you should also get in touch with your local police department and find out if you need a permit to hold your rally. If you do need a permit, you should apply for it as soon as possible, as it may take many weeks for it to be approved.

Who Will Come?

One of the main goals of your rally is to show popular support for your issue or cause. Getting many people to come to your rally is the best way to do this. As you get closer to the day of the rally, hopefully many people in your **community** will hear about it and attend. However, you should also encourage many people you know to attend as well. Ask your parents, family members, and friends to show up and support you and your cause.

You may also want to ask adults who know a lot about your cause to come speak at your rally. At your rally against drunk driving, for example, you might ask someone who works at the police department to come speak about why it's so unsafe. You could also ask a drunk-driving victim to give a short speech about her experience. Organizations like MADD also have both experts and ordinary **volunteers** who are willing to speak to crowds about drunk driving.

Signs and Slogans

One of the most important parts of your rally is getting people to show up. However, once people arrive, you will want to keep their attention and share as much information about your cause as possible. There are many things that you can do to make your rally effective and engaging to the public. Larger rallies and marches sometimes use floats and musicians to attract attention.

If you are holding your rally in one location, try using colorful signs, public speakers, and chants to get people's attention and share information.

If you have asked people to speak at your rally, think about what they might need. For example, should they speak from some sort of stage or raised platform? Will they need microphones to be heard in large spaces? If so, you may need things such as speakers and electrical outlets. Make a list of everything you will need and check each item off as you plan. Be sure you have everything you need before the day of the rally!

If you have been to a rally or seen photos of one, you probably noticed many people holding signs. Signs are an easy way to share a message with many people at once. First, think of a **slogan**, or a word or phrase that gives the main idea of your cause, to write on your sign. For example, a sign at a rally to stop drunk driving and encourage safe driving might read Stop Drunk Driving or A Designated Driver Saved My Life. Good slogans are usually short and create a strong image or idea in people's heads.

To make your signs, visit a local arts and crafts store or supermarket to get your supplies. You will want to get poster board, markers, paints, and any other art supplies you might need. You might find it fun to invite some friends over and make signs together. One person might have neat handwriting, while another may be great at coming up with catchy slogans!

Get the Word Out!

When the details of when and where your rally will be are set, it is time to spread the word. Tell everyone you know about the rally and ask everyone to tell other friends as well. **Flyers** are a great way to get the word out, too! Be sure to include the date, time, and location of your rally. You should also include some information about the cause to get people interested in the issue. If you are able, you might also want to include a photo or illustration.

Once you have your flyer designed, ask an adult to help you make many copies. Then post the flyers in places all over your neighborhood and town. You might post them at local grocery stores, libraries, churches, and schools. Try to think if there are any places where people might have a special interest in your cause. For example, for your rally against drunk driving, you might post flyers near restaurants and bars in your town. Wherever you decide to post flyers, always get permission from the owners of the property or business.

RALLY TO STOP DRUNK DRIVING!

WHEN: Thursday, April 9th
WHERE: Town Square
WHY: To keep people safe on the roads we share!
WHAT TO BRING: Yourself, a sign, and a friend!

The Big Day

When the day of the rally arrives, it is time to step into action. Get to the rally location early to greet people as they arrive. Be sure to bring all of your supplies, including signs, microphones, and information sheets, with you. If you were told to get a permit for the rally, bring that with you as well.

DESIGNATED
DRIVERS
SAVE
LIVES!

As your rally begins, people passing by may stop and ask questions about what is going on. You might find it helpful to ask a few volunteers to stand close to where people are passing. As people stop, these volunteers can answer questions, share more information about the cause, and hand out the information sheets you printed. Remind your volunteers to be polite.

Sometimes a rally will get the attention of people who do not agree with the cause. If anyone comes to your rally and is rude or mean to you or your volunteers, stay calm. Continue to be polite and focus on sharing information. However, if you ever begin to feel unsafe, tell a parent or police officer.

As your rally goes on, try to keep things moving. You can try leading the crowd in a chant in support of the cause. You can also ask a few volunteers to take turns leading the chants. Like a slogan, a chant should be short and express the main point of your rally. For example, the slogan Safe Driving Saves Lives would work well as a chant.

As your rally comes to a close, take the opportunity to thank people for coming. Remind them once more about the importance of supporting your cause. Encourage them to do more research, talk to their friends about the issue, or even write a letter to a local elected official about the cause.

When the rally is over and you are ready to leave, make sure you have taken everything you brought. If the crowd at your rally left any trash, be sure to clean it up and leave the place the way you found it.

27

Making Connections

The main purpose of a rally is to show support for a cause and spread useful information. A rally can have another important purpose, though. It can also connect you with others who care about the same cause you do. The people who attend rallies generally believe strongly in a cause and want to create change in their schools, communities, or country. By talking to people and making connections at your rally, you can create a **network** of supporters who are willing to stay involved and take action.

At your rally, get contact information for anyone who would like to get involved in your cause. Consider passing around a piece of paper on which people can write down their email addresses. Email is a quick and easy way to share information with many people and stay in touch. You could even create and email a monthly newsletter that includes updates and new information.

29

Following Up

Organizing an effective rally is a big job. When your rally is over, send thank-you cards to anyone who volunteered and helped out. You could also send thank-you cards to a business owner who let you use her parking lot or a local police officer who helped you apply for a permit. Thank-you cards may not seem like a big deal, but they are a great way to let people know you appreciate their help.

Holding a rally is just one step to creating change and supporting a cause. If you feel very strongly about an issue, stay involved! Learn all that you can about the issue and keep up with new information. Another step may be writing to an elected official or giving a speech at your school. Find as many ways as possible to make your voice heard!

Glossary

assemble (uh-SEM-bel) To gather a group together.

awareness (uh-WER-nes) Knowledge of what is going on around you.

Bill of Rights (BIL UV RYTS) The first 10 amendments to the US Constitution.

city council (SIH-tee KOWNT-sul) A group that makes laws for a city.

community (kuh-MYOO-nih-tee) A place where people live and work together or the people who make up such a place.

flyers (FLY-erz) Pieces of paper displayed publicly to make the public aware of events happening or things for sale.

network (NET-wurk) A system or group of things that connect to each other.

permit (PER-mit) Written permission to do something.

research (rih-SERCH) Careful study.

slogan (SLOH-gin) A word or a phrase used by a group to tell others its main idea.

suffrage (SUH-frij) The right of voting.

volunteers (vah-lun-TEERZ) People who offer to work for no money.

Index

C
cause(s), 5–6, 8, 12, 16–18, 20–22, 25–26, 28–30
change(s), 6, 28, 30
community, 16, 28

F
freedom(s), 4, 7

G
government(s), 6, 8, 11–12

I
information, 5, 11–12, 18–19, 21–22, 25, 28–30

issue(s), 5, 8–12, 14, 16–17, 21–22, 26, 30

L
law(s), 5–6, 11–12

M
meeting, 5, 9
movement(s), 6–7

N
network, 28
newspaper, 9–10

O
organization(s), 5, 11, 17, 21

P
permit, 12, 15, 24, 30
purpose, 5, 14, 28

R
research, 10, 17, 26
rules, 5, 15

S
slogan(s), 20–21, 26
suffrage, 6

U
United States, 4, 6

V
volunteers, 17, 25–26

Websites

Due to the changing nature of Internet links, PowerKids Press has developed an online list of websites related to the subject of this book. This site is updated regularly. Please use this link to access the list: www.powerkidslinks.com/beacl/rally/